Tennis

Have you ever wondered what it must be like to play on the Centre Court at Wimbledon? This book captures the thrill and suspense of the tennis court, and lets you into some of the top tennis players' secrets about how to win matches. You can also find out how to learn and improve your game.

InterSport

Tennis

Bryan Cutress

Colour photographs by
All-Sport Limited

Wayland/Silver Burdett

1040

InterSport

The world of international sport seen
through the cameras of some of the world's
greatest sports photographers, showing in
action both children and the stars they
admire.

Cycling	Motorcycling
Golf	Soccer
Gymnastics	Tennis
Ice Sports	Track and Field

Frontispiece **Watch the Ball!** – Jimmy Connors of the
USA demonstrates the first law of tennis . . . watch the
ball right on to the face of the racket . . . and then attack
it!

First published in 1980 by Wayland Publishers Limited
49 Lansdowne Place, Hove, East Sussex BN3 1HF, England
© Copyright 1980 Wayland Publishers Limited
ISBN 0 85340 772 X

Published in the United States by Silver Burdett Company, Morristown, New Jersey
1980 Printing
ISBN 0382 06425–9

Phototypeset by Trident Graphics Limited, Reigate, Surrey
Printed in Italy by G. Canale & C.S.p.A., Turin

Contents

What the stars think of the game

Billie Jean King is probably the most successful woman tennis player of all time. She has won a record number of titles at Wimbledon, and has taken the U.S. Open Championship, and the French, Italian and Australian Championships in her long career as a top class tennis player.

'Why do you enjoy tennis?' I asked Billie Jean King.

'Because tennis is a magnificent sport,' she replied. 'It's healthy, and good for meeting lots of people. It gives plenty of satisfaction when it is properly played and there is an almost unrivalled chance to travel. What more can you ask of a sport?'

'A top tennis player can now afford to retire at about 22, but they don't because they love the game,' she continued. 'Unless you love tennis, don't bother trying to become a champion. You must enjoy yourself enough to be able to bounce back after losing an important game and work even harder after it.'

Next I asked my all-time favourite, Australia's Lew Hoad, who was once a Wimbledon

Reach for the Sky – The racket is flung high to announce that Bjorn Borg of Sweden has won yet another Wimbledon singles title. Most men would content themselves with winning the Wimbledon title once – but Borg had just won the most sought after title in men's tennis for the fourth year running.

champion and also winner of the French, Italian and Australian Championships.

'The beauty of tennis,' he said, 'is that you can play it from the age of four until you are 80, and you need only one other person for a game. It keeps you active and all you need is a racket and a couple of balls. To become a champion, though, you have to sacrifice a lot and work hard. It takes a long time to know whether you are going to be any good, unless you are a prodigy like Bjorn Borg, Ken Rosewall, or John McEnroe.'

Finally I asked Frank Sedgman, Wimbledon champion in 1952, why he is still playing.

'Because it's a great game,' he answered. 'It keeps me fit, has taken me all over the world and provided me with a good living.'

A Study in Determination – Billie Jean King, perhaps the greatest woman tennis player of all time, stretches for a backhand return at Wimbledon.

The structure of world tennis

Tennis was first played in England, then in Europe and America, and now it is played all over the world. The International Tennis Federation is the world governing body. There are now 108 member countries and tennis has become the third most widely played sport in the world.

The Federation is responsible for the promotion and development of the sport. It frequently arranges training courses for young people who live in the underdeveloped countries of the world and it runs top team competitions, like the Davis Cup and the Federation Cup.

Until 1972, the International Tennis Federation was all-powerful, but then a group of famous players including Cliff Drysdale, Arthur Ashe, John Newcombe and Stan Smith formed the Association of Tennis Professionals. This was the first players' union. The Women's Tennis Association was formed in the following year. The Association of Tennis Professionals and the Women's Tennis Association have grown in size and strength so that now nothing happens in the

In the Hot Seat – Top players today compete for large sums of money, and disputed line calls all too often lead to ugly scenes on the court. Some players would do well to remember that the officials help to make Wimbledon and the rest of the world's major tournaments tick.

America's Cup! – Another success for the American girls. Their Federation Cup team collects the trophy after beating the Australians at Eastbourne in 1977. America and Australia have dominated the Federation Cup since it was started in 1963. Only two other countries have ever won the Cup – South Africa in 1972 and Czechoslovakia in 1975.

professional game of tennis without the approval of these unions.

The players' strike during the 1973 Wimbledon Championships made it clear that the union and the Federation were heading for a battle that might wreck the game. So in 1974 the two sides got together and formed the Professional Council. This is made up of three representatives from the Association of Tennis Professionals, three from the Federation, and three from the tournament promoters. The Professional Council now decides how the world's major championships are going to be run.

Wimbledon

Wimbledon's centre court is one of the most famous and most exciting sports arenas in the world. The most thrilling matches have been played out on the centre court, holding the fourteen thousand-strong audience spellbound. Every year, many thousands of people enter a ballot hoping to win the right to buy a couple of centre court tickets, but only a small number of them are successful.

It is not only the centre court that makes Wimbledon the most important tennis tournament in the world. The organization of the championships is superb. On the first day of the championships, at exactly two o'clock, everyone is in his seat and the reigning men's singles champion steps on to the centre court. As soon as the electric scoreboards show that the first point has been won, the rest of the matches on the other seventeen courts begin. A total of about 590 matches will be played and 14,400 balls

The Gladiators Emerge – Bjorn Borg and Roscoe Tanner enter the Centre Court arena at Wimbledon before the 1979 men's singles final. The photographers battle for the best view.

The Home of Tennis – Anyone who has ever hit a tennis ball would surely love to play once on Wimbledon's famous Centre Court. This court attracts 17,000 spectators a day during the Championships.

used before the championships come to an end. It may surprise you that so many balls are used but next time you watch a game played at Wimbledon, notice how many times the umpire asks for new balls.

Wimbledon lasts for only twelve days each year, during the last week in June and the first week in July. There are 270 umpires and hundreds of officials who make sure that everything runs smoothly. Then of course there are the ball boys (though there are actually ten girls among the ball 'boys') who have a very important part to play, gathering up the balls during games and keeping the players supplied. More than 300 journalists from all parts of the world are provided with courtside seats, writing rooms, a restaurant and a closed circuit television centre.

Did you know that all this went on behind the scenes?

Young and Old in Waiting – A netcord judge waits for the telltale quiver that shows a 'net', which means that the player must serve again, while a ballboy waits to collect a 'netted' serve.

The Wayward Genius – Ilie Nastase of Romania *(left)* has never won the men's singles title at Wimbledon, yet during his hey-day he was undoubtedly the most exciting player in the world. His final against Stan Smith of the USA in 1972 will be remembered as one of the greatest ever seen at Wimbledon. Since that defeat, his career has been littered with a trail of fines, suspensions and controversial incidents – as well as many glorious victories!

17

Other major championships

Wimbledon's reputation for being the best organized and most important tournament in world tennis is being hotly contested by two other major championships – the U.S. Open and the French Hard Court Championships.

Since it was first held at the new National Tennis Centre at Flushing Meadow in New York City, the U.S. Open has had more room for spectators on its centre court, which can hold 19,200 people. There is also more prize money to be won in the U.S. Open than there is at Wimbledon.

The centre court seating at the French Championships, held at Stade Roland Garros in Paris, was increased to 18,000 in 1979, 2,000 more seats than at Wimbledon. There is also more prize money.

There are a few drawbacks to these tournaments, however. In America, the championships take place over thirteen days at the end of August and beginning of September. At this time, New York is usually hot and humid and the noise of aircraft flying low overhead to nearby La Guardia Airport is particularly irritating for the players. In

The 'Slow' Stuff – But not if you or I were facing a professional's serve! This red clay court at Stade Roland Garros in Paris is more suited to the player who has sound ground strokes than to the player with raw power.

18

Paris, a player needs patience because many of the matches on the 'slow' dusty courts last more than three hours. Hard courts, such as those in the French Championships, are 'slower' to play on than grass courts, such as those in England and in Australia. Sound ground strokes are more important than power on hard courts, and a player needs to be fit and very skilful to win the French title. The championships last for fourteen days in May/June.

But despite more prize money and more spectator accommodation, the U.S. Open and the French Hard Court Championships are still not as popular with the players as Wimbledon.

Wimbledon, the French Championships and the U.S. Open have always been the world's major events in tennis, but the Australian Championship completes the quartet which makes up the 'Grand Slam'. Very few players win the Grand Slam in the same year. Only Australian Rod Laver has achieved it twice, as an amateur in 1962 and as a professional in 1969.

The Young Pretender – Tracy Austin, at the tender age of seventeen, is already pushing Martina Navratilova and Chris Evert Lloyd for the coveted number one position in women's tennis. She has been so successful that she could hang up her racket now and never have to worry about earning another cent in her life!

Double Tops! – John McEnroe and Peter Fleming of America were the 1979 Wimbledon doubles champions – an incredible achievement for so young a pair.

The Grand Prix

John McEnroe turned professional in June 1978 and by the end of the year, he had earned nearly a quarter of a million pounds (half a million dollars). Almost all of this came from the Grand Prix circuit.

The tennis Grand Prix is the richest Grand Prix of any sport. The circuit of 90 tournaments is worth £5½ million (over $12 million) in prize money. It attracts all the world's leading male players.

Championship matches for the Grand Prix go on all over the world in 28 different countries. Each event is graded according to the prestige and prize money it offers. So Wimbledon, the U.S. Open and the French and Australian Championships are found in the top group. Those worth only between £25,000 and £37,000 ($55,000 and $81,400) are in the bottom group.

Ambition fulfilled! Martina Navratilova had won countless tournaments on the women's Grand Prix circuit, but her greatest ambition was to win the Wimbledon singles title. This picture was taken after the Final in 1978. No prizes for guessing if she won or not! She won again in 1979.

As in the motor racing grand prix, competitors are awarded points for their success in each event. The events go on throughout the year, and at the end of the circuit the leading eight players compete in The Masters' Tournament. The winner claims a large prize and the top 50 share in the bonus pool.

To be eligible for the bonus pool, a player must compete in at least 20 Grand Prix tournaments in a year. In 1978 this rule put out Jimmy Connors, who had only competed in 13 events, and Bjorn Borg, who had competed in 14. And they finished in the top two places!

There is a Grand Prix for women, too, but this involves only 40 events and there is less prize money. Star players in this circuit are Chris Evert Lloyd and Martina Navratilova.

Perfect Positioning –Manuel Orantes of Spain shows how footwork is essential for good tennis *(left)*. Fitness and the ability to 'be in the right place at the right time' can make the difference between a good player and an 'also-ran'.

Men's championships

More than 50 countries compete each year for the World Men's Team championship or the Davis Cup, as it is better known. It is one of the biggest international team competitions in sport and it has been a regular part of the tennis calendar since 1900 when an American, Dwight Davis, donated the silver cup. It is the most exciting team competition in world tennis. At first, the only challengers for the cup were Britain and America, but in 1904, France and Belgium joined the fray and soon other countries were competing.

Throughout the year, the competition is played on a knock-out basis. The format of the matches is two singles on the first day, doubles on the second and the reverse of the first day's singles on the third. Every player wants to represent his country in the Davis Cup, even though it is a very nerve-racking experience and often less financially rewarding than other tournaments.

All the old and new star names have appeared in the Davis Cup records – past champions such as the Doherty brothers, Fred Perry and Donald Budge and new stars

Mind Over Matter – The world champion – Bjorn Borg. Borg was still a teenager when he helped his country win the Davis Cup in 1975. It's often said that there are more naturally talented players than Borg, but when it comes to winning close matches – where mind has to triumph over matter – Borg is usually the master.

The Destroyer – John McEnroe of America destroyed Britain's chances in the 1978 Davis Cup Final in Palm Springs, California. Already he was being tipped as the man most likely to take the title 'the world's greatest' from Bjorn Borg.

like Jimmy Connors, Bjorn Borg and John McEnroe. The most successful country is America, but it is only narrowly leading over Australia. Only five of the other 61 countries who have tried to win the cup, have succeeded – Britain, France, South Africa, Sweden and Italy.

The only other competition like the Davis

Never Say Die – If you can't run to the ball – throw yourself at it. Try to get it back at all cost as there is always the chance that your opponent will 'give' you the point by making an easy mistake – while you're lying on your back staring at the heavens!

Cup is the King's Cup which is a European indoor championship, played during the first two months of each year. It began in 1936 as a knock-out event, but it changed to a league competition in 1976. Each match lasts one day, during which two singles and one doubles are played. It is good training for the more demanding Davis Cup.

Women's championships

The first World Women's Team champion-ship was held in 1963 when the Federation Cup was launched at Queen's Club in London. Each match is made up of two singles and one doubles, and the competition is played at one centre during one week.

Britain's Virginia Wade is the record holder for the number of matches played in the Cup. She has made more than 80 appearances and won over half of her matches. Billie Jean King has made less appearances – only 60 – but she has won 90% of her matches.

It is again America and Australia who have dominated the Federation Cup, just as they dominate the Davis Cup. The only other winners have been South Africa and Czechoslovakia.

There is one other women's team competition and this is the Wightman Cup. It is an

The Will to Win – Virginia Wade *(left)*, mainstay of Britain's Federation Cup team, showing the determination and aggression that has won her so many matches.

annual event in which America and Britain compete. Every year they fight it out, with the Americans usually coming out on top. Britain has won it only ten times since 1923, when Hazel Wightman donated the cup and so started the contest. Many say that the contest for the Cup is too one-sided and that a European team should be allowed in, or else the competition should be scrapped. But just as the campaign to change the Wightman Cup gathers momentum, a spectacular match like the one in 1978 occurs. Then Britain snatched victory from the Americans in the last match of the tie, thrilling 6,000 spectators and mass television audiences all over the world.

The Queen of the Courts – Grace, power and beauty are all illustrated as Chris Evert Lloyd *(left)* plays her famous two-handed backhand from the base line.

Junior championships

It is hard to believe that Tracy Austin was still a junior when she won the U.S. Open title in 1979. This little Californian, who picked up her first racket when she was two and appeared on the front page of a tennis magazine a couple of years later, has set the pace for the rest of the world's junior players.

It will be difficult for anyone to match her. In 1977, when she was only 14, she was the youngest to get a place in the American top ten ranking, the youngest to play at Wimbledon and the youngest to win a professional singles title. But for those aspiring young players, there are plenty of ways to improve your game – one of which is to watch a master player like Tracy Austin!

Other ways of improving your game are to enter various competitions. In Britain and America, there are national championships for different age groups: Under 12s, 14s, 16s and 18s. There are also junior team and individual events on an international scale.

Britain probably has the most junior championships. Hard court championships are held at Wimbledon in September each

Opportunity Knocks! – The spread of junior tournaments such as those sponsored by Pepsi-Cola is creating opportunities for young players throughout the world, like Hana Mandlikova of Czechozlovakia *(left)*, to enjoy more competition. This raises playing standards as well as strengthening the bonds of international friendship.

year, indoor championships are held in London in January, and grass court competitions take place at Eastbourne in August. In addition, there is the junior invitation event which is run alongside the Wimbledon Championships, and is open to the world's top young players.

The invitation event is part of the Pepsi junior series, which includes nine tournaments held in various countries, ending with the World Championship Final in Florida in February of each year. In the 1978 Final, a second Tracy Austin burst on to the tennis scene. It was Andrea Jaeger, a tiny thirteen-year-old, who came on as a substitute and ended up taking the Pepsi title. This was one of the memorable moments that make tennis such an exciting sport to watch. It was also very encouraging for young players – it is obviously not only strength that brings success – it is courage, determination and skill.

Watch Out Tracy! – Andrea Jaegar *(left)* was 13 years old and a tiny 4ft 9in tall when she won the 1979 Pepsi-Cola Junior International Championship against a girl five years her senior. The Americans seem to have an endless production line of young outstanding players.

Equipment

If you look closely at the tennis stars, you will notice how smart they always look. They spend a lot of time choosing what they will wear so that they are comfortable on court and also have the best equipment to help them win. Manufacturers of tennis rackets and tennis clothes pay stars to wear and use their products as it is good advertising for them. So the players have a wide choice.

Beginners should also be careful to choose what will help their game. Choosing the racket is the most difficult task, and a professional's advice would be most useful before you buy your racket – so ask at your local club if possible. You can pay anything from £7 ($16) to £180 ($400) for the Slazenger Phantom. Obviously, the cheapest is little more than a toy and the most expensive only for the professional. A good price to pay for a beginner's racket is about £15 ($33). It will have synthetic strings but when you have reached a reasonable standard, you can replace these strings with real gut at an additional cost of another £15 or so.

You should notice the grip and weight of

Gut Reaction? – John McEnroe keeps a careful eye on the tension of a racket that is being restrung. Different players play with rackets strung to different tensions. Natural gut is almost always used by professionals, but nylon is advised for beginners as gut is very expensive . . . it takes fourteen days and the intestines of seven sheep to make one set of gut for a tennis frame!

How's That? – A youngster gets help and advice on how to grip the racket. It is very important to play with a racket that is the right weight and size.

your racket. Naturally the size and weight you are will make a difference; the most important thing is to feel comfortable with the racket in your hand.

Expensive tennis balls are the best buy as they last longer.

As far as clothing is concerned, there are

In Style – Victor Pecci of Paraguay, seeded number 8 at the 1979 Wimbledon Championships, shows not only style in his serving action, but also in his clothes. Tennis equipment is now very big business indeed, with many different manufacturers seeking the 'name' of big stars to promote their equipment. Clothing in particular has been revitalized since the strict rules about all-white clothing were relaxed a few years ago.

so many good tennis clothes manufacturers that you can just go for the most comfortable. Recently, the rule about wearing all white has been relaxed and some colours have been introduced. Buy all your equipment from a good sports shop.

Matchplay

Most experts of the game agree that Bjorn Borg has less pure talent for hitting a tennis ball than John Lloyd. So what makes Borg an all-time great and Lloyd just one of the rest? It is all a matter of mental strength, pride and unshakable determination. Borg possesses all of these qualities in abundance and this is what makes him the star.

At the age of 15, he startled the world of tennis by beating the experienced New Zealander, Onny Parun, after losing the first two sets. This was his Davis Cup début.

Borg does not freeze or play safe when facing up to an important point. In fact, no one can tell from his behaviour whether he is worried or not when he is game point or even match point down. This frequently unnerves his opponents.

Two other players with similar temperaments to Borg are Rod Laver and Chris Evert Lloyd, neither of whom has been seen to throw a tantrum whatever situation faces them. This is unlike some competitors – we have all seen Nastase showing his feelings at critical moments in matches.

An Early Interest . . . could pay dividends. Great tennis players have one thing in common – their love for the game. This young sideline judge will learn a great deal from watching older players.

42

He Who Waits – A young player, Hans Simonsson of Sweden, waits for his oppponent to serve. He blows on his racket hand to dry any perspiration to make sure that the racket doesn't twist in his hand under the impact of the serve. It is also very likely that he does it to steady his nerves!

It is usually the sign of a great player not to appear to be affected by the critical moments, when in danger of losing a hold on the match. Many players motivate themselves in one way or another. Billie Jean King can be seen talking angrily to herself, urging herself on, and Jimmy Connors stalks about the court and slaps his thigh as he gets psychologically ready for the big points.

One feeling all great players share is a

When Something Goes Wrong – The great Ilie Nastase has never been one to hide his feelings. Some players like Bjorn Borg keep their emotions very much to themselves. Others – well, they just *have* to let their feelings be known!

desire to win. Wherever they are playing, tennis stars want to win. The coaches know that there is little to choose between the basic skills of the top hundred stars in international tennis and that the only real difference between the winners and the losers is strength of character. This is something a coach cannot teach you. Without it, the best stroke player in the world does not get to the top.

Scoring

The scoring in a game of tennis is 15, 30, 40 and with the next point you have won the game. If the players reach three points each the score is called 'deuce' and the game goes to the first player to win two successive rallies.

When a player does not score a point in a game this is referred to as love.

A racket is spun to decide who will serve first and after that the service alternates between the two players, each serving for one complete game.

A player gets two chances on each point to get his serve into the service court and if he fails on both, he has produced a double fault and loses the point.

If a player takes six games and has a clear lead of two games he has won the set but if the score reaches six-all a tie-break game is usually played.

The tie break game is comparatively new to tennis and to win it a player has to take seven points with a lead of two clear points. If five points all is reached the game continues until one player has a two points lead.

Down But Definitely Not Out! – Two sets down but still fighting. Borg launches himself into a topspin backhand during the third set of his great tussle against Mark Edmondson in the second round of the 1977 Wimbledon Championships. With five sets to play in men's tennis, a player can lose the first two sets hopelessly, and yet still be in with a chance of winning the match. Borg managed to beat Edmondson.

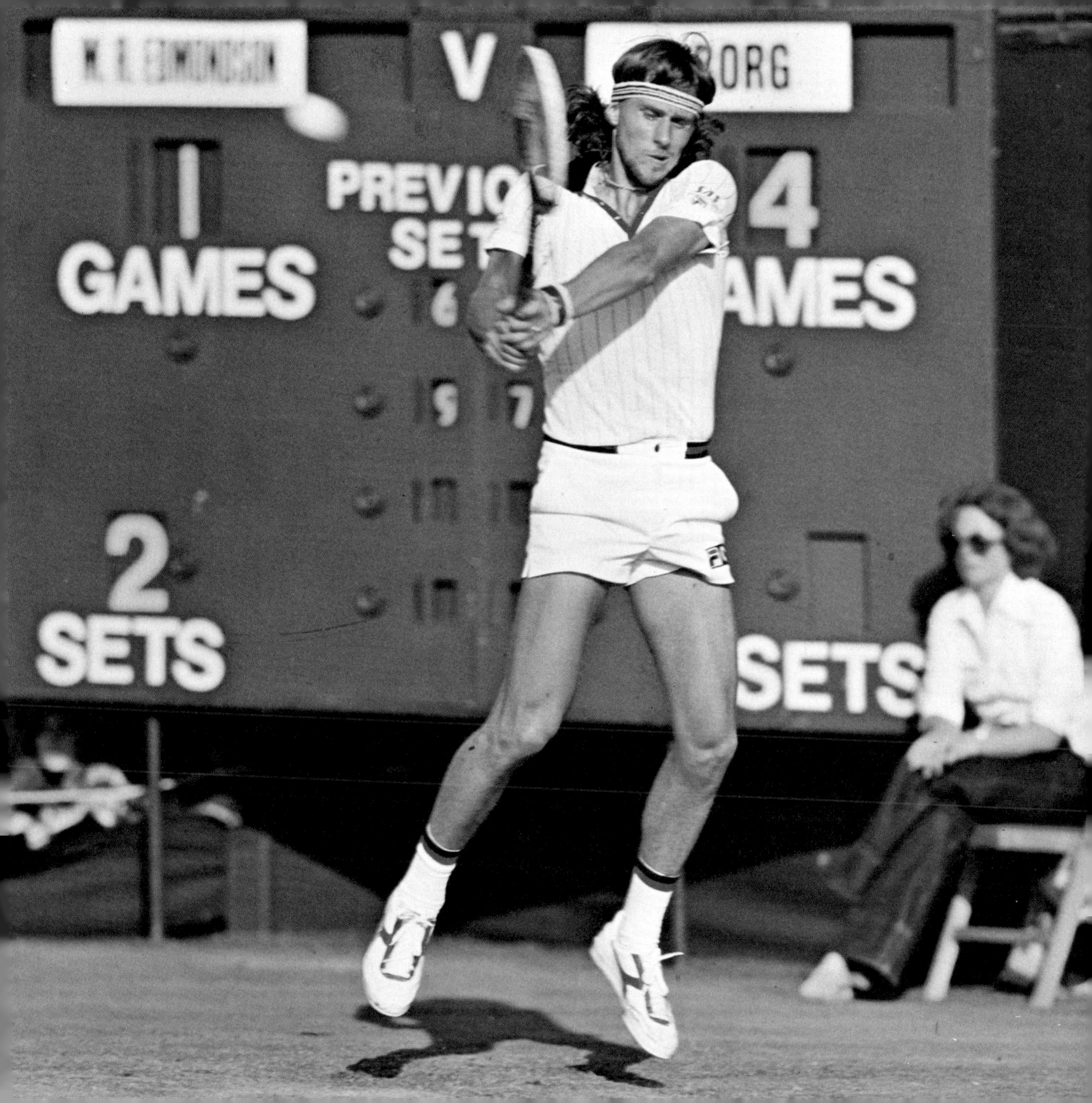
V
1
GAMES
2
SETS
4
SETS

Keeping the Crowd in Touch – The Wimbledon scoreboard registers the score during a match between Gottfried and Ramirez *(far end)* and Fleming and McEnroe – two of the greatest doubles partnerships in the world. There are also scoreboards outside the Centre Court, and during very popular matches, huge cheering crowds have been known to gather round just to read the scoreboard. Such is the attraction of tennis!

Learning the Ropes – No flashy gear for this young player *(left)*, just an eye on the ball and the desire to serve an ace. Serving is a very important part of the game of tennis. Brilliant servers like Roscoe Tanner of America can win a game without their opponent even touching the ball!

In No-Man's Land – This club player has found himself having to play a ball from the middle of the court. It is easier to smash or volley a ball if you are near to the net.

The tie-breaker was introduced to prevent exceedingly long matches which between two powerful servers, can often be very boring.

Sponsorship

Many large companies in the world give money to sports. Some splash out huge sums on one particular event or series of events. Some prefer to put their cash into the development of the game. Others help out simply by employing sports stars.

Among the leading tennis supporters are Volvo, the Swedish motor-car company, World Championship Tennis, an American group owned by a millionaire, and Avon, a cosmetics company. All three run a series of tournaments and between them pour about £3 million ($6.6 million) a year into tennis.

Saab, another Swedish car manufacturer, used to sponsor the King's Cup, but now devotes its money, in Britain at least, to the juniors. It is committed to supporting junior international matches, tournaments and a scholarship scheme over the next five years.

B.P. organize an international Under 21 team tournament in Hamburg and, more important, a tennis fellowship which runs tournaments and sets up 'clinics' each year in England, Scotland, Wales, Barcelona, Teheran, Istanbul, Beirut and Paris. At

All Eyes on the Player??? – The crowd applauds a well hit forehand, yet how many of them are also noticing the SAAB sign on the advertising hoarding in the background without realizing that they are doing so?

Early Starter – Just one of the youngsters likely to benefit from Saab's sponsorship of the junior game.

these clinics, many of the stars – like Ken Rosewall, Rod Laver, John Newcombe, Mark Cox and Ann Jones – spend time coaching and encouraging young players.

The Prudential Insurance Company sponsors all the British junior championships. They also organize the senior county championships which are played at 22 centres around Britain.

So you can see that sponsorship is a very important part of the tennis world, and that without it the game and the players would suffer.

The Greatest of All Time? – If Rod Laver hadn't chosen to turn professional after winning Wimbledon for the second time in 1962 he might have won more Wimbledon singles titles than any other player in history. He returned to Wimbledon in 1968 winning the title that year and the following year. He is the only man to have won the 'Grand Slam' twice, which means that he won the Wimbledon, French, American and Australian titles in the same year on two occasions.

How much money in the game?

Tennis is one of the most financially rewarding sports in the world.

Not only is there a yearly total of about £6 million ($13.2 million) available in prize money for men and about £4 million ($8.8 million) for women, but all the leading players are paid a great deal of money by sports goods manufacturers if they wear and use their products. Bjorn Borg, for example, is supposed to have been given more than £1 million (over $2 million) for signing a contract to use one particular make of racket, and he is paid a fortune to wear certain makes of clothing.

All in all, players like Bjorn Borg and Chris Evert Lloyd – that is, the real stars of the game – are already millionaires.

The men have the opportunity to earn the most money. Some of the prizes offered at major tournaments are absolutely staggering amounts of money. For instance, the World Championship Tennis Final, an event for eight players in Dallas each Spring, offers £125,000 altogether ($275,000), with £50,000 ($110,000) for the winner. And the

Still Flying at Over 35! – Tom Okker, the 'Flying Dutchman' earned over £50 (over 100 dollars) for every *game* he played during an Over-35 tournament at the Royal Albert Hall in London! The major tournaments offer greater rewards – the Wimbledon men's singles winner in 1979 collected £20,000 (nearly 50,000 dollars) and you can win even more than that!

Britain's Hope – Sue Barker is one young British player likely to 'succeed' in women's tennis. Sue has already made a small fortune through playing tennis, and she could achieve even greater success.

W.C.T. Tournament of Champions in Forest Hills, New York, is the world's first quarter of a million pounds (over half a million dollars) tournament with £150,000 ($330,000) in prize money for individual players and £100,000 ($220,000) in the bonus pool, which the 50 top players share.

Even in the Veterans' Tournament at the Royal Albert Hall in 1979, Tom Okker

One Who Can Afford to Clown – Tennis millionaire Jimmy Connors amuses the crowd during a Wimbledon doubles in which he partnered the 'court-jester' supreme, Ilie Nastase.

beat 51-year-old Pancho Gonzales in the final and picked up £4,000 ($8,800). This means that Tom Okker earned at the rate of £500 (over $1000) for a set or £54 ($119) for a game. Top women players earn well over £50,000 ($110,000) and women's champion Martina Navratilova earns over twice this amount. Sue Barker won £18,000 ($39,000) in one tournament week!

Tennis in the eighties

Who will become the stars of the Eighties? Some of the present day ones are bound to keep in the top league – like John McEnroe and Tracy Austin. The boys who should mature into stars during the decade are Ben Testerman and Scott Davis, two teenagers from America, who should help America to keep a grip on the Davis Cup. Then there is Yannick Noah, a Frenchman who was discovered when he was only ten by Arthur Ashe. Ivan Lendl of Czechoslovakia and Per Hertquist of Sweden are also names to watch out for.

The girls who should make it to the top are American Mary Lou Piatek, Czechoslovakia's Hana Mandlikova and Regina Marsikova, and Lena Sandin of Sweden.

What of the game itself? It seems certain that the leading players will compete in fewer tournaments during the next ten years and prefer to save their efforts for the less tiring but equally rewarding exhibitions despite the opposition of all the sport's governing bodies.

Double-handed players will be seen more

The One to Beat – Tracy Austin will almost certainly be the player that the others will have to beat during the Eighties.

Ashe's Discovery – Yannick Noah of France *(left)* was discovered in the Cameroons in 1971 by Arthur Ashe (who won the Wimbledon singles title in 1975). Noah will almost certainly be one of the stars of the Eighties.

often as the young people who modelled themselves on Chris Evert Lloyd, Bjorn Borg and Jimmy Connors move into their late teens.

There may be a take-over of the profitable side of the game by powerful managers of the players. This is becoming a more serious threat. But whatever happens at the top, there will continue to be plenty of encouragement of young players, in schools and clubs.

Triples?! – There is no such game, but coaches often put three of their pupils at each end to make sure that as many as possible are actively involved during a training session. *(right).*

Index

All pictures by All-Sport Photographic Ltd., except on pages 40, 43, 50, 51 & 53 (Timothy Eagan, Susan Griggs Agency); pages 36, 41 & 44 (Tommy Hindley); and pages 20 & 21 (Duomo).